Presented

to

_____

on_____ _____

by_____

DEVOTIONALS
FOR NURSES

DEVOTIONALS FOR NURSES

Rhoda Snader Lapp, R.N.

Baker Book House
Grand Rapids, Mich.

Copyright 1974 by
Baker Book House Company

ISBN: 0-8010-5539-3

Printed in the United States of America

I SOLEMNLY
PLEDGE MYSELF
before God and in the presence
of this assembly
to pass my life in purity and to
practice my profession faithfully.
I WILL
abstain from whatever is deleterious
and mischievous and will not take
or knowingly administer
any harmful drug.
I WILL
do all in my power
to maintain and elevate
the standard of my profession
and will hold in confidence
all personal matters
committed to my keeping
and all family affairs
coming to my knowledge in the practice
of my calling.
With loyalty
WILL I
endeavor to aid
the physician in his work,
and devote myself
to the welfare
of those committed to my care.

The Florence Nightingale Pledge

Preface

God is so good! Praise His Name!

Because God helped me to plan the contents of this book, I want to dedicate this book to the honor and glory of God.

My prayer is that God will richly bless each one of you as you serve Him by meeting the spiritual as well as the physical needs of your patients.

Rhoda Snader Lapp, R.N.

Contents

From Thee
    all skill and science flow,
    all pity,
        care,
            and love,
    all calm and courage,
        faith
           and hope;
O pour them from above.

Charles Kingsley

Your word is a lamp to guide me,
and a light to my path.

Ps. 119:105, TLB

1 God's Light

Walking in the darkness can be very hazardous indeed. Without light to illuminate the way, we may stumble, lose our bearings, or twist our ankles by stepping into ruts or holes. And for those who have night duty in darkened rooms or halls, bumping into objects can be an ear-splitting experience.

When a lantern or flashlight is held low, the rays of light very quickly dispel the darkness at our feet and we can take one step after another, safely. We can also see the little side paths which follow almost directly parallel to the main path at first but ultimately lead in a much different direction.

Similarly, when God's Word serves as our guide in our daily walk, our lives are influenced and directed by the principles found in that Book. We will be aware of the pitfalls and evils of alluring by-paths — temptations which come clothed in harmless-looking packages and seem to be only a little off dead center of the path. It is easy to spot the out-and-out temptations without using

So shall my walk be close with God,
Calm and serene my frame;
So purer light shall mark the road
That leads me to the Lamb.

the searchlight of God's Word. It's the so-called little things that cause us to trip and stumble. Remember what the Bible has to say about one being faithful in little things?

To be efficient nurses we need to know and follow the principles of nursing which are set forth in textbooks of medical and surgical nursing. To be victorious Christians, living successfully for God, we must know and use the principles which God has given to us in His textbook, the Bible.

As Christian nurses we have a two-fold obligation: first, to walk in the light, and second, to reflect and share that light with others. How bright is your light? Recharge your batteries daily as you let God's Word speak to you and direct your life.

PRAYER: Dear God, thank You for the Bible which reveals the path to joyful living now and to eternal life hereafter. Help me to be willing to share this light with others. Please forgive me when I fail to do this. Amen.

15

O Lord,
thou hast searched me,
  and known me.
Thou knowest my downsitting
  and mine uprising,
thou understandeth my thoughts
  afar off.

Ps. 139:1, 2

2 God's X rays

God does not need man's x-ray equipment to peer deep into the inner recesses of our lives, or to know what is wrong with us spiritually. He has special x rays, the kind that man will never be able to duplicate. We do not need to pose in any special position to have God x-ray us. It is not necessary to hold still until the x-ray technician clicks the button. The films do not need to be developed and read before God can make a diagnosis of our physical or spiritual illnesses. God does it all instantly.

He knows our downsittings (our resting times), and even what we are thinking of during these free moments. He knows our uprisings (our working hours) and how we are performing on the job, be it good or bad.

Men or women may be able to deceive people but they'll never be able to pull the wool over God's eyes. "For the eyes of the Lord search back and forth across the whole earth, looking for people whose hearts are perfect toward him, so that he can show his great power in helping them" (II Chron. 16:9 *TLB*).

For those of us who are Christians and living for the Lord, it is indeed a great comfort to know that God can see us all the time and can send His protecting and sustaining power according to our needs.

Be aware that God's x-ray beams shine straight through to our minds and hearts, revealing to Him our most secret thoughts. "He knows about everyone, everywhere. Everything about us is bare and wide open to the all-seeing eyes of our living God; nothing can be hidden from him to whom we must explain all that we have done" (Heb. 4:13, *TLB*).

PRAYER: Dear God, help me always to remember that "Thou God seest me." Help me to keep these words in mind as I plan my daily activities, my leisure time, and my quiet time. Forgive me, Lord, when I become lax in this area. Amen.

3 How to Deal with Frustrations

I'm sure that almost all nurses would agree that the rewards of nursing certainly far outweigh the frustrations we encounter. To have a part in helping someone recover from an illness, injury, or surgery is a wonderful privilege indeed. For those whose recovery is impossible from a medical standpoint, we can endeavor to keep them as comfortable as possible until God performs a miracle or calls them home to be with Him. Here, too, we have an opportunity to demonstrate a sympathetic attitude toward the patient and his family while they are going through this very trying experience.

But who is there among us who has not had a frustrating day at one time or another? Maybe you've had a very demanding, uncooperative patient. Maybe you've been extremely short of help because someone called in sick and there was no replacement for that person. Maybe for some reason or another a tired, overworked doctor complained about something that wasn't even your fault. Or, maybe it was one of those days when the supervisor was on the warpath about very trivial things. Perhaps all of these things happened on the same day. As a result, by the time you finally got off duty you were ready to scream and to pull your hair out of your head. Then what should you do? Or, what did you do?

We need to give vent to our feelings in a constructive way. When I was a student and I thought I couldn't take the tensions anymore, I'd go to my room in the dorm,

God is our refuge
and strength,
a very present help in trouble.

Ps. 46:1

hold a pillow tightly over my mouth, and scream away without hurting anyone's eardrums. Talking over your frustrations with an understanding person always gives relief. Many is the time my roommate and I by just simply unloading our pent-up emotions to each other were able to relieve tensions. A sympathetic listener is of great value. Since I've married, my husband lends a sympathetic ear and I try to do the same thing for him.

Some people find relief by going for a brisk walk. This is not ideal, however, for a nurse with tired feet. Pounding on typewriter or piano keys helps others to get rid of their frustrations. If you feel at home in the kitchen, try kneading some bread dough. That may yield double dividends.

We should by all means tell the Lord about our troubles and depend on Him for our strength. We are told, "Let him have all your worries and cares" (I Peter 5:7, *TLB*).

The story is told of a weary traveler carrying a heavy sack which he had thrown over his shoulder. Someone came along and offered this individual a ride in a horse-drawn wagon. The man accepted the ride but continued to keep the heavy burden on his shoulder instead of putting it on the wagon. How ridiculous!

PRAYER: Dear Lord, help me to cast my burdens, cares, and frustrations on You. And, Lord, don't let me pick them up again. Amen.

Dear Brothers, How can you claim that you
belong to the Lord Jesus Christ, the Lord of
glory, if you show favoritism to rich people
and look down on poor people? If a man comes
into your church dressed in expensive clothes
and with valuable gold rings on his fingers,
and at the same moment another man comes in
who is poor and dressed in threadbare clothes,
and you make a lot of fuss over the rich man
and give him the best seat in the house and
say to the poor man, "You can stand over there
if you like, or else sit on the floor," — well,
judging a man by his wealth shows that you are
guided by wrong motives.

James 2:1-4, TLB

4 No Respecter of Persons

How do you react when a definitely unkempt patient is brought into the hospital for medical care? He may reek with an offensive odor from a lack of cleanliness. He may have rotten decayed teeth. He may have a skin color different from yours. To top it all off, he may also be crude and irritating. Do you feel disgusted and repulsed? Would you just as soon be assigned to someone else who is clean and cultured and well-mannered?

Well, he's your patient. So what are you going to do about it? You can do what you have to do without reaching out to this human being and pat yourself on the back for doing your job in a professional manner. Or —

> *We hand folks over to God's mercy,*
> *and show none ourselves.*
>
> George Eliot

Perhaps if you keep in mind that this person, filthy and uncouth though he may be, has an eternal soul, you may be able to be more tolerant of his filth, stench, and manner. Christ died also for this individual. He would have had compassion on this patient and you claim to be an imitator of Christ. Can you do less?

"How can you claim that you belong to the Lord Jesus Christ . . . if you show favoritism to rich people and look down on poor people?"

PRAYER: Lord, help me to treat all people alike, even when it is extremely difficult to do so. Amen.

Behold,
the Lord's hand is not shortened,
  that it cannot save;
  neither his ear heavy,
  that it cannot hear.

Isa. 59:1

5 God's Stethoscope

Just as a doctor listens to the heartbeats of his patients to discover their cardiac problems, or to their lungs to determine the nature of their pulmonary disorders, so God listens to our heart cries so He can come to our rescue when we are in distress.

God wants us to tell Him about the things that make us happy and to thank Him for them. He also wants us to come to Him with both our large and trivial problems. If anything at all is bothering us, He wants us to talk it over with Him.

A physician's answer to a patient's need varies according to the illness. And the Great Physician's answers to our prayers are varied according to our circumstances.

Sometimes He in His great love for us answers, "No," because He is wiser than we are, and He in His foreknowledge knows that what we've asked for would not be good for our well-being.

Sometimes God's reply in answer to our prayers is,

Jesus, my strength, my hope,
On Thee I cast my care;
With humble confidence look up,
And know Thou hearest my prayer.

Charles Wesley

"Wait awhile." It may well be that the ideal time to have the request fulfilled has not yet arrived. I can truly thank God for some delayed answers to my prayers; the delays were for my own good.

Many, many times God's answer to our prayers is, "Yes." Parents want to give good things to their children and God also delights in giving us, His children, good things.

So if you pray and your prayers are not answered immediately, keep in mind that God has a reason for every kind of answer He gives us. And He has our ultimate good in mind each and every time. He is just that kind of a God. Praise His Name!

PRAYER: Dear God, thank You for always having time for me. Thank You for being interested in hearing about both my joys and sorrows. Thank You, too, for all Your answers to my prayers. Amen.

*Is anything too hard
  for the Lord?*

Gen. 18:14

6 God Can Do Anything!

What are your needs and desires?

Do you have financial difficulties? marital problems? failing health? an unsaved friend or relative?

For every problem there is a solution in the Bible. God is able "to do far more than we would ever dare to ask or even dream of — infinitely beyond our highest prayers, desires, thoughts, or hopes (Eph. 3:20, *TLB*). Go to God and confidently expect help from him.

Peter needed money for taxes. Jesus told him to go fishing, open the mouth of the first fish he caught, and use that money to pay taxes for both Jesus and Peter. Now, don't rush off and buy a fishing pole but do ask the Lord for wisdom and help to solve your financial difficulties.

Read Ephesians 5:22-31 to learn what Paul has to say about marriage. That won't be an instant cure for your marital woes, but it does put things in the right perspective.

Maybe your world is turned upside down by a serious, perhaps incurable, illness. Tell the Lord about

I have no cares, O blessed Lord,
For all my cares are Thine;
I live in triumph, too, for Thou
Has made Thy triumphs mine.

your fears and worries and give Him that burden. Instantly His peace will come upon you. Perhaps He'll heal the sickness. Perhaps not. But through it all you can and will have a serene spirit and you will experience an awesome measure of His sustaining power. I know, I can speak from experience.

Tell the Lord, too, about your unsaved friend or relative. Keep on praying for that soul. God's timetable is different from yours and you have no reason to be impatient. Your job is to pray, to trust, and to keep on witnessing.

"Oh, what a wonderful God we have! How great are his wisdom and knowledge and riches! How impossible it is for us to understand his decisions and his methods! For who among us can know the mind of the Lord?" (Rom. 11:33, 34, *TLB).*

PRAYER: Thank You, Lord, for being greater than I am. Amen.

My help cometh from the Lord,
  which made heaven and earth.
He will not suffer thy foot to be moved:
  He that keepeth thee
    will not slumber.
Behold, he that keepeth Israel
  shall neither slumber
    nor sleep.   Ps. 121:2-4

7 Night Duty

Some nurses call the eleven-to-seven shift the grave-yard shift. Possibly one reason is that, in spite of all the endeavors put forth by the most competent medical team, often the seriously ill or the critically wounded patients do not live to see the early morning light. When patients are prepared to meet their Lord and Maker, what better way is there to graduate from this earth to heaven than to slip quietly away during the stillness of the night?

During the night while the majority of the patients are sleeping and most of the people in the world outside the hospital walls have ceased their daytime labors, have turned off their lights, and are enjoying a good night's sleep, it is a comfort to know that the Lord is wide awake; He never sleeps. We are not alone in our vigil during the night hours, for the Lord is tenderly watching us from above.

Often when I am on night duty or even driving alone in the darkness, I think of the verse: "For thou wilt light my candle: the Lord my God will enlighten my darkness" (Ps. 18:28).

Eventually there will be a time when we will not need light from candles or any other sources. ". . . and they need no candle, neither light of the sun; for the Lord God giveth them light: and they shall reign for ever and ever" (Rev. 22:5). The same text tells us, "And there shall be no night there. . . ."

Since we are not in heaven yet, and since the number of crimes committed increases during the darkness of night, let us claim the Bible verse of the psalmist: "I will both lay me down in peace, and sleep: for thou, Lord, only makest me dwell in safety" (Ps. 4:8).

For those who are on night duty, perhaps we could paraphrase this verse and say, "I will drive to work in the darkness in safety, with my doors all locked, and the headlights on my automobile working properly. I will walk safely from the hospital parking lot into the hospital entrance, and will be on duty in peace, for thou, Lord, only maketh me to dwell in safety."

PRAYER: Thank You, dear Lord, for being concerned about the safety of Your children. Amen.

But God showed his great love for us
by sending Christ to die for us
while we were still sinners.

Rom. 5:8, TLB

8 God's Great Love for Us

Has anyone ever asked you, "How can a God of love ever send a soul to suffer in hell fire for ever and ever?"

Jesus tells us in Matthew 25:41 that hell was prepared for the devil and his angels. Christ went on to tell us that those people who do not care for Him or His words will also go to everlasting punishment. But the righteous shall inherit eternal life.

Jesus can make this promise because by His suffering, death, and resurrection, He has redeemed all those who believe in Him. He doesn't want any creature to go to hell "but that all should come to repentance" (II Peter 3:9).

However, we are creatures of free choice and God won't compel us to repent, believe, and be baptized. It's up to us to choose our eternal destiny, be it heaven or hell.

Consider the love God and His Son have for each of us. What a great sacrifice was made for our benefit.

But here within my trembling hand I bring
  This will of mine — a thing that seemeth small.
But Thou alone, O Lord, canst understand
  How when I yield Thee this, I yield mine all.

Certainly the Father would have preferred to have His Beloved Son with Him in heaven those thirty-three years Jesus was on earth. And Jesus Himself would have preferred the splendor of heaven to this earth.

God is merciful and loving but He is also just. And because God's justice demanded that a price should be paid for our sins, someone must pay that penalty. The only one who could meet all the demands of God's law was His own Son. God gave *His very own Son* to satisfy for our sins so that by Christ's atonement we could be reconciled to God and become His children. What incredible love!

Christ willingly assumed the role of Redeemer. He could have refused to die that horrible, cruel death. But He didn't. He loved us too much for that. What priceless love!

PRAYER: What language shall I borrow to thank Thee, dearest Friend? Lord, let me never outlive my love to Thee. Amen.

Jesus saith unto him,
 I am the way,
   the truth,
and the life:
no man cometh unto the Father,
   but by me.

John 14:6

9 The Way to Heaven

How would you answer a dying person's question, "What must I do to be saved?" Or, "How can I go to heaven?" You may be confronted with that question sooner than you think.

You as a Christian nurse will want to seize that opportunity to explain efficiently and quickly the way of salvation to one who has postponed until the very end of his life a decision regarding his eternal destiny.

Use that New Testament the Gideons gave you when you were still a student. It fits nicely in your uniform pocket. Jot down some references in the inside front cover:

John 3:16 "For God so loved the world, that he gave his only begotten Son, that whosoever believeth in him should not perish, but have everlasting life."

Romans 10:9 "That if thou shalt confess with thy mouth the Lord Jesus, and shalt believe in thine heart that God hath raised him from the dead, thou shalt be saved."

Romans 10:13 "For whosoever shall call upon the name of the Lord shall be saved."

> *O Saviour, I have nought to plead,*
> *In earth beneath or heaven above,*
> *But just my own exceeding need,*
> *And Thy exceeding love.*
>
> Jane Crewdson

I John 1:9 "If we confess our sins, he is faithful and just to forgive us our sins, and to cleanse us from all unrighteousness.

Ephesians 2:8 "For by grace are ye saved through faith; and that not of yourselves: it is the gift of God."

Better yet, memorize these verses. But keep your Bible handy because the patient may want to see those soul-saving words for himself.

I don't need to remind you that your daily ministrations to your patients will be a loud and clear signal to them about the caliber of your Christianity. If you radiate joy and peace along with a special brand of care and compassion, you may be asked by patients who intend to live for a while, "What do you have that I don't have?"

Be ready for that too.

PRAYER: Father, let me be aware of the spiritual needs of my patients. Bless my efforts to win souls. Amen.

Be thou faithful unto death,
and I will give thee
a crown of life.

Rev. 2:10

10 A Crown of Victory

Remember how thrilled and how happy you were to receive your nurse's cap? Since nursing schools vary in their capping procedures, we may not all have had the same capping ceremonies. But we all received it — our crown of victory — somewhere along the way.

In the nursing education course I followed, we had to successfully complete two very full and extremely difficult semesters of college work before we ever got to wear any of our nursing attire or to go on the hospital wards for strictly supervised duty.

Perhaps some of you had capping exercises with candlelight and organ music. I attended one of these delightful services for a friend of mine. Whatever the procedure you followed to acquire your nurse's cap, I'm sure you consider it a real crown of victory. Perhaps you received a black band for your white nurse's cap when

> *God will not look you over for medals,*
> *degrees, or diplomas,*
> *but for scars.*

Elbert Hubbard

you became a senior student nurse. I was thrilled to receive that black strip. It was mine to wear forever on this earth.

But I am even happier to know that in heaven I'll replace my nurse's cap with a crown of gold! That will surely be infinitely far more rewarding than receiving my nurse's cap, including the black velvet band.

PRAYER: Dear God, my heart is overwhelmed because of Your great goodness and abundant blessings. Even though I studied hard and worked diligently, I give You the thanks and praise for helping me to successfully conquer all those difficult exams, including those tough state boards. Thank You for the privilege of wearing a crown of victory now and for the promise of a crown of gold in heaven. Amen.

Give us this day our daily bread.

Matt. 6:11

11 God's Nutrition

Jesus knows that we need food for our physical existence. Therefore He taught His disciples (and us) to pray, "Give us this day our daily bread." Jesus was not condoning laziness here. Rather He was acknowledging a dependence upon God. Paul remarked: "For even when we were with you, this we commanded you, that if any would not work, neither should he eat" (II Thess. 3:10).

Even when we work we are still dependent upon God to supply our food. There is always the possibility of a famine or a food shortage. However, it is so comforting in the light of these possibilities to read the words of Jesus: "So my counsel is: Don't worry about things — food, drink, and clothes. For you already have a life and a body — and they are far more important than what to eat and wear. Look at the birds! They don't worry about what to eat — they don't need to sow or reap or store up food — for your heavenly Father feeds them. And you are far more valuable to him than they are . . . So don't worry at all about having enough food" (Matt. 6:25-31, *TLB*). What a soothing message!

When we leave this world and its cares behind and enter the Glory World, we will enjoy even more of God's nutrition for we are told: "To everyone who is victorious, I will give fruit from the Tree of Life in the Paradise of God" (Rev. 2:7, *TLB*). I wonder what kind of fruit that will be. Most certainly it will be even more luscious than the sweetest, juiciest peach or pear or

Bread of heaven,
feed me till I want
no more.

W. Williams

orange! Those who may not be overly fond of earthly fruit will certainly enjoy this wonderful heavenly fruit.

There will be twelve different kinds of fruit in heaven. I would say that's quite a variety. That is so typical of our kind and loving God. "And he shewed me a pure river of water of life, clear as crystal, proceeding out of the throne of God and of the Lamb. In the midst of the street of it, and on either side of the river, was there the tree of life, which bare twelve manner of fruits, and yielded her fruit every month" (Rev. 22:1, 2).

We will also partake of the hidden manna of heaven. We will find out more about this heavenly manna when we get there. "To him that overcometh will I give to eat of the hidden manna" (Rev. 2:17).

In heaven we will not need to worry about a food shortage, food poisoning, indigestion, or being overweight. We will be out of the reach of spiraling food prices due to inflation. Restricted, unpalatable diets will be a thing of the past, forever! Hallelujah!

PRAYER: Dear God, thank You for Your great goodness. Thank You for caring for me here below and for the wonderful heavenly nutrition that I will be able to enjoy to the fullest, without any restrictions, in my heavenly home. Amen.

*And God shall wipe away
all tears from their eyes;
   and there shall be no more
         death,
   neither sorrow, nor crying,
neither shall there be any more pain:
   for the former things are passed away.*

Rev. 21:4

12 No Illness in Heaven

Even if I didn't believe the Bible to be true, I would be convinced that there is a heaven because of the expression of rapture I've seen on the face of one of the patients I had when I was a senior student nurse. Other nurses and doctors gathered around the bedside of this gentleman to give what help we could. But we all knew he was beyond medical help. And the patient knew his time on earth was fast drawing to a close. His breathing was so shallow and his pulse and blood pressure so faint that we could not detect either one. When we turned him over we could see that he no longer had any circulation in his legs; they were those of a dead man. Yet, he was conscious and the expression on his face was glorious to behold. I believe he was seeing something marvelous that his weakened condition would not allow him to describe to us.

From sorrow, toil, and pain,
And sin we shall be free;
And perfect love and friendship reign
Through all eternity.

John Fawcett

One of my friends was doing private duty nursing for a dear Christian friend whom we both knew personally. He was dying. She told me that his face was glowing with rapture and joy as he passed away. She knew he was seeing something great and wonderful. In his dying moments he could not tell her about it because he was too weak and exhausted.

Another Christian friend died of cancer. She died with a smile on her lips. Those of us who work with terminal cancer patients know very well that there is nothing in this devastating disease, often accompanied by excruciating pain, that would create a smile for the patient.

PRAYER: Dear Father, thank You for the promise of a glorious home and a new body — free from sickness, pain, and deformity — in heaven. Amen.

And the building of the wall of it
        was of jasper:
and the city was pure gold,
        like unto clear glass.
And the foundations of the wall of the city
        were garnished with all manner
                of precious stones.

Rev. 21:18, 19

13 The Beautiful City of Heaven

John painted many word pictures of heaven. The description of the New Jerusalem in Revelation 21:18-21 is almost beyond human comprehension. I've read through the list of the twelve foundations many times without trying to understand or imagine what John is telling us. Recently I consulted a Bible dictionary *(Davis)* and came up with this list of gorgeous colors in the foundation:

	Stone	*Color*
1	jasper	yellow, green, or red
2	sapphire	transparent bright blue
3	chalcedony	pale blue or gray
4	emerald	rich green
5	sardonyx	white and orange-brown
6	sardius	transparent red or brown

When I stand before the throne,
Dressed in beauty not my own,
When I see Thee as Thou art,
Love Thee with unsinning heart,
   Then, Lord, shall I fully know,
   Not till then, how much I owe.

Robert M. McCheyne

7	chrysolite	pale olive green or gold
8	beryl	blue-violet or yellow and brown
9	topaz	yellow
10	chrysoprasus	apple green
11	jacinth	amber
12	amethyst	purple or blue-violet

Keep in mind that this magnificent foundation supported a wall of jasper and that the wall enclosed a golden city. There were twelve gates, each one a solid pearl, through which one entered the city. What dazzling beauty! Small wonder that my dying friends departed this life with a radiant, rapturous glow.

PRAYER: Dear Lord, my heart is overwhelmed when I think of all the splendor in heaven that is awaiting me. Hallelujah! Amen.

He shall reward every man
according to his works.

Matt. 16:27

14 God's Diary

I still have the diary I started during the years of my nursing education. It is quite interesting and sometimes a bit amusing to read the little incidents that would have been forgotten had I not recorded them. I recorded feelings about certain tests and exams, as well as some of the duties and happenings of the day, both pleasant and unpleasant.

I've also recorded some of the experiences of my courtship days. One day Lois (a fellow classmate) and I with eager anticipation carefully planned every detail of a perfect picnic for our dates. Alas, we discovered after we were way out in the country that we had forgotten to take a knife to cut the watermelon. All that planning, and we goofed! We wanted to make a good impression on our dates. Anyway, we ended up using a nurses' bandage scissors to cut that melon.

God will not ask thy race,
Nor will he ask thy birth;
Alone will He demand of thee,
What hast thou done on earth?

There are probably many other small interesting incidents in life that I've forgotten simply because I didn't record them. But not so with God. He is keeping an accurate record of all our earthly deeds. Some day we will receive a reward for all the many deeds of kindness we have done and are doing. Even such a small act of a Christian giving a cup of cold water will not go unnoticed. I'm sure we've all done many long-forgotten deeds of kindness, even going the second mile many times, which are recorded in heaven for us.

While we should not do deeds of kindness to others for our own benefit, yet rewards do follow our deeds.

PRAYER: Dear Father, thank You for keeping an accurate record of my life. Help me to be aware of the small, often unspoken needs of others and then to serve them for Your sake, without thought of reward. Amen.

Lay not up for yourselves
treasures upon earth,
where moth and rust doth corrupt,
and where thieves break through and steal:
But lay up for yourselves treasures
in heaven,
where neither moth nor rust doth corrupt,
and where thieves do not break through
nor steal.

Matt. 6:19, 20

15 The Bank of Heaven

The story is told of a wealthy man who refused to help his own daughter to buy a house because he was so stingy. He did not want to lose any interest on his precious money. But alas! He lost every penny of his fortune shortly thereafter because of a bank failure caused by the depression. What a tragedy!

The bank of heaven has no need for a vault, a combination lock, a timed lock, concealed cameras to photograph the activities of robbers, or even a burglar alarm. It is not affected by a drop in the stock market or a depression. The bank of heaven is completely reliable and the interest rates are high and secure.

Jesus said: "Sell that ye have, and give alms; provide yourselves with bags which wax not old, *a treasure in the heavens that faileth not,* where no thief approacheth, neither moth corrupteth" (Luke 12:33, italics

We make a living by what we get,
but we make a life by
what we give.

added). And, "Go and sell that thou hast, and give to the poor, and thou shalt have treasure in heaven" (Matt. 19:21).

The late Dr. Harry Rimmer just a few days before he died wrote to Dr. Charles E. Fuller: "You say, brother, that next Sunday you are going to preach about Heaven. I am interested in that land as I have a piece of property there. I didn't buy it, for the Savior purchased it for me with His own blood. For 55 years I have been sending up material, out of which the great Architect Jesus Christ is preparing a place for me."

Where is your treasure?

PRAYER: Dear Jesus, thank You for Your words of wisdom. Help me to heed them. May I not set my eyes and heart on things that quickly fade away. Amen.

. . . hear, . . . listen to what the Spirit
  is saying to the churches:

Everyone who is victorious . . .
I will give to each a white stone,
and on the stone will be engraved
  a new name
that no one else knows
  except the one receiving it.

Rev. 2:17, TLB

16 A New Name

Remember how thrilled you were when you had the blessed privilege of changing your name from your maiden name to your married name? What a privilege it was to take the same last name of the man you love with all your heart. (If you are still single, you are probably still dreaming of that big day in your life.)

Name pins were so important in our student nurse days. The head nurse sent me off duty to get my name pin one day when I had forgotten to wear it. She would not tolerate any new, unidentified students working on her floor.

And then there was that progressive change of initial identification following my name, first the change from S.N. (Student Nurse) to G.N. (Graduate Nurse) after I graduated, and then finally to R.N. (Registered Nurse) after I passed state boards. I'll never forget the thrill I experienced the day the nursery supervisor said to me, "You are now a R.N." The hospital school of nursing had just been notified that I had passed state boards.

> *High is the rank we now possess;*
> *But higher we shall rise;*
> *Though what we shall hereafter be*
> *Is hid from mortal eyes.*

Isaac Watts

The same welcome news was in my mail box when I got home.

When we get to heaven we will all have a new name. I wonder what mine will be. I imagine it will have some musical connotation and I expect to be pleased with it because everything in heaven will be exceedingly wonderful.

Even though the Bible does mention, "On the stone will be engraved a new name that no one else knows except the one receiving it," and even though we will be transformed into heavenly beings in heaven, yet we will somehow retain our earthly identity. We are told in I Corinthians 13:12, "Then shall I know even as also I am known."

PRAYER: Dear Father, I thank You that I will receive a new name in heaven and that I will also know my friends, relatives, and patients who have gone on to be with You in that land of indescribable beauty. Amen.

Yet even there in Sardis
some haven't soiled their garments with
     the world's filth;
they shall walk with me in white,
    for they are worthy.
Everyone who conquers will be clothed in white,
    and I will not erase
    his name from the Book of Life,
but I will announce
    before my Father and his angels
        that he is mine.

Rev. 3:4, 5 (TLB)

17 White Raiment

How proud I was at graduation when I publicly wore my white professional uniform for the first time. I was so glad to discard those bluish-grey and white striped uniforms with their detachable white collars and cuffs and white pinafores. At last I could wear an all-white, crisp and sparkling uniform.

White stands for cleanliness, purity, and victory. We are promised that in heaven we will have white raiment that will never become tattered or torn or even soiled. In heaven everything will be pure and undefiled.

There is another text that talks about white raiment: "Then I heard again what sounded like the shouting of a huge crowd, or like the waves of a hundred oceans crashing on the shore, or like the mighty rolling of great thunder, 'Praise the Lord. For the Lord our God, the Almighty, reigns. Let us be glad and rejoice and honor

46

> *And they who, with their Leader*
> *Have conquered in the fight,*
> *Forever and forever*
> *Are clad in robes of white.*

Bernard of Cluny

him; for the time has come for the wedding banquet of the Lamb, and his bride has prepared herself. She is permitted to wear the cleanest and whitest and finest of linens.' (Fine linen represents the good deeds done by the people of God.)" Rev. 19:6-8, *TLB*.

The bride is a symbol for the Church. The Church includes every one of us who have been washed in the blood of Jesus. We also have our names written in the Book of Life. And we will be given personal recognition when Jesus announces before the Father and His angels that we are His. What a glorious moment that will be!

PRAYER: Dear Jesus, help me always to remember to ask You to cleanse me of my sins through Your shed blood. You have loved me with such an overwhelming love. Amen.

And took care of him.

Luke 10:34

18 First Aid

The Good Samaritan not only rendered first aid; he also assumed the role of the ambulance driver. Of course the ambulance was the donkey. It was not equipped with a screeching siren or flashing red lights.

Since there were no hospitals in that vicinity in that era, the Good Samaritan did the next best thing. He took his patient to the inn. And there he took care of him. He did private duty nursing and he may even have worked a double shift. The amazing thing about it is that he was not paid for his services. After all, his patient had just been robbed and had no money. Even more amazing is the fact that the next day the Good Samaritan paid the innkeeper two pence, which was equivalent to two days' wages. To top it all off, he said to the innkeeper, "Take care of this man. Don't discharge him until he's well. And, I'll pay you the balance."

We have good reason to believe that the man who was traveling on the crooked, narrow road, down through rocky passages, was a Jew. Robbers who were known to lurk in these concealed places had taken his clothes and his money, beat him up, and then left him half dead. A priest came along, took a good look, and passed by on the other side of the road. A Levite, a person who served in the Jewish temple, came along, looked, and then he too passed by on the other side of the road. Finally the Good Samaritan arrived.

Even if it's a little thing,
  do something for those who have need of help;
something for which you get no pay
  but the privilege of doing it.

For generations the Jews and the Samaritans had been bitter enemies. Getting down off his donkey, the Samaritan knelt beside the injured man, an enemy. The Good Samaritan was certainly in a good position to be clobbered by any bandits who may have been hiding behind the rocks.

What would you have done? Would you have taken time to check the area carefully first, to see if it was safe to climb off your donkey and to get in a kneeling position?

What would you do today if you saw an injured, beat-up person, yes, even an enemy, lying along the shoulder of the highway? Would you quickly step on the accelerator so the same bandit who harmed this person wouldn't have a chance at you? Would you try to hush your conscience by calling the police and/or the ambulance? Or would you render first aid and assist the helpless victim until he was able to take care of his own needs?

PRAYER: Dear Jesus, thank You for this lesson of love. Help me to always keep in mind that as I treat others so I am treating You, for You have said, "Inasmuch as ye have done it unto . . . these . . . ye have done it unto me." Amen.

A new heart also will I give you,
   and a new spirit
     will I put within you:
   and I will take away
     the stony heart
   out of your flesh,
and I will give you a heart of
   flesh.

Ezek. 36:26

19 God's Heart Transplants

Heart transplants are relatively new to the medical profession. Way back in the Old Testament times God talked about spiritual heart transplants.

When the Great Physician performs His spiritual heart transplants, He has no need of a preoperative scrub, sterile gown, mask, or gloves, an anesthesiologist, surgeons to assist Him, operating room nurses or technicians, sterile instruments, or even sutures. The patient does not require preoperative medication. Neither is he troubled with postoperative discomforts such as nausea, vomiting, or pain. And he receives a new heart rather than an already used one. His new heart will last him through all eternity. Furthermore, the cost of God's

O kindle, Lord most holy,
  Thy lamp within my breast
To do in spirit lowly
  All that may please Thee best.

heart transplant is not calculated in terms of dollars and cents.

One thing is parallel in both types of heart transplants and that is the willingness of the patient to submit to the procedure. In the hospital the patient has to sign an Operative Permit before he has surgery. All that God asks of us is that we be willing to accept this new heart that He offers to us.

PRAYER: "Create in me a clean heart, O God; and renew a right spirit within me." Thank You for the uncomplicated procedure that You, the Great Physician, are able to use. Amen.

The blood you have placed on the doorposts
will be proof that you obey me.

Exod. 12:13, TLB

20 There's Life in the Blood

We all know that in order to sustain physical life, we need to have an adequate amount of blood flowing through our circulatory system. If for any reason a great blood loss occurs, an immediate blood transfusion is necessary or death will occur. Therefore, there's life in the blood.

The above text, however, is not concerned with the mechanics of a transfusion, but rather with the mechanics of being protected by the blood. God gave the Israelites specific instructions to follow to avoid a visit by the angel of death at their homes. "Then Moses called for all the elders of Israel and said to them, 'Go and get lambs from your flocks, a lamb for one or more families depending upon the number of persons in the families, and kill the lamb so God will pass over you and not destroy you. Drain the lamb's blood into a basin, and then take a cluster of hyssop branches and dip them into the lamb's blood, and strike the hyssop against the lintel above the door and against the two side panels, so that there will be blood upon them'" (Exod. 12:21, *TLB).*

The lamb and the blood were excellent Old Testament pictures or symbols of the promised Messiah.

Immortal love of Thine,
Thy sacrifice,
Infinite need of mine
Fully supplies.

Mrs. Merrill E. Gates

Because Christ shed His blood for us, we can be spared the agony of spiritual death. When Adam sinned, man became separated from God; and this sinful nature was transmitted from one generation to another. "By one man sin entered into the world, and death by sin; and so death passed upon all men, for that all have sinned" (Rom. 5:12).

Just as the blood of the passover lamb in Egypt was the substitute for the blood of the firstborn, so Christ's atoning blood is our substitute. "Thou wast slain and hast redeemed us to God by thy blood" (Rev. 5:9).

When we accept the atoning blood of Jesus, He forgives us and we are justified (it is just as though we never sinned!) by His blood. "Being now justified by his blood, we shall be saved from wrath through him" (Rom. 5:9). God will not even remember our sins. Since God forgives us for our sins through the atoning blood of His dear Son, we ought to forgive ourselves and forget about our past, after we've made any necessary restitution.

PRAYER: Father, thank You for the atoning, life-giving blood of Your Son. Amen.

Thou shalt not kill.
    Exod. 20:13

21 The Abortion Issue

One day a nineteen-year-old girl came into our office (I presently work for a private physician) carrying a six-week-old baby. I have never seen a young girl look so pitiful, so haggard and utterly miserable. She offered no explanation for her look of despair. I did notice from the chart that she was married. After the doctor had seen her and the baby, I had a free moment. I glanced through her medical history to see if I could find a clue to that terrible look of anguish. I discovered she had had an abortion earlier while she was still single. Post-abortion guilt is not uncommon. Perhaps looking into this baby's face reminds her of her firstborn who was destroyed by means of an abortion. I wonder if she would recommend having an abortion to anyone else.

In the light of the above Bible verse, what should be our advice to anyone who may consult us about having an abortion?

The majority of our scientists today are telling us that life begins at conception — that unknown moment when the sperm and the egg unite. That life will continue until death occurs, no matter where that death takes place: inside or outside the walls of the uterus.

Silence is no certain token
That no secret grief is there;
Sorrow which is never spoken
Is the heaviest load to bear.

Frances Ridley Havergal

I hope the Lord will have mercy on those who are saying that a fetus is not an actual human being until quickening occurs or until the baby is born. If that statement is a fact, why are some of these fetuses being reserved for human research? Why are they not discarded immediately?

What advice will you give when you are asked about the wisdom of having an abortion? Will you merely describe the various procedures available to accomplish abortion? Will you give your personal reasons, valid though they may be, for not seeking an abortion, and leave it at that? Or will you spend some time with the questioner, counseling her and pointing her to God's Word. This is really a golden opportunity! Use it — for the sake of the mother, the child, yourself, and God's glory.

PRAYER: Father, help me to keep my antennas tuned for cries for help which may come in various ways. Give me wisdom when I deal with those who are considering an abortion. Give me the right words, an open ear, and a compassionate heart that does not hastily judge another. Amen.

From the rising of the sun
  unto the going down of the same
the Lord's name is to be praised.

Ps. 113:3

22 Praising the Lord

Praising the Lord "from the rising of the sun unto the going down of the same" certainly indicates very clearly that we are to be praising the Lord, or to be in a thankful spirit, during the time that we are going about our daily duties, whether they be during the day or night.

Praising the Lord is a good antidote for depression because it causes depression to vanish quickly, like darkness is dispelled in the presence of light. I have discovered that if when I am depressed, I concentrate on the Lord's goodness to me, either by writing on paper or making a mental list of all the things I have for which to be grateful, my depression quickly disappears. Praising has such a tremendously uplifting effect on the one who praises.

In heaven we will spend a lot of time praising the

O Lord! that lends me life,
Lend me a heart replete with thankfulness!

Lord. John writes: "Then in my vision I heard the singing of millions of angels surrounding the throne and the
Living Beings and the Elders: 'The Lamb is worthy'
(loudly they sang it!) ' — the Lamb who was slain. He is
worthy to receive the power, and the riches, and the
wisdom, and the strength, and the honor, and the glory,
and the blessing' " (Rev. 5:11, 12, *TLB).*

So let's have a little bit of heaven on this earth by
praising our Wonderful God who richly deserves our
praises for many things, including the greatest gift of all
— the gift of His Son.

PRAYER: Dear God, I praise You and thank You for
all the manifold blessings You shower upon me daily.
Help me to maintain a thankful spirit even when the
situation I'm facing may not be pleasant. Amen.

I will instruct thee and teach thee
in the way
which thou shalt go;
I will guide thee with mine eye.

Ps. 32:8

23 Divine Guidance

To be guided by the will of God is a gentle, not a forced, guidance. It presupposes that we are looking to God for guidance. We must be looking directly at a person before he can guide us with his eyes. And then we must be willing to receive guidance or instruction, for an unwilling pupil is not a good student. The verse: "In all thy ways acknowledge him, and he shall direct thy paths" (Prov. 3:6), indicates also that we should take the initial action by acknowledging God in everything we plan and then He will give us His direction.

God does not stand over us with a billy club in His hand, bellowing in our ear, "You must do thus and so." He is, however, interested in even the smallest detail of our lives and doesn't want us floundering around in bewilderment wondering what our next move should be. He is concerned about whom we marry, where we work, where we live, and how we use our time and talents.

How can you know what God's will is in specific

Teach us, in every state,
To make Thy will our own.

A. M. Toplady

areas? Hannah W. Smith in *The Christian's Secret of a Happy Life* says: "There are four ways in which He reveals His will to us — through the Scriptures, through providential circumstances, through the convictions of our own higher judgments, and through the inward impressions of the Holy Spirit on our minds. Where these four harmonize, it is safe to say that God speaks."

I know from personal experiences that God does, if we allow Him, give personal direction in our lives. Because He made us, He knows what is best for us. His guidance is not restrictive; it leads to a happy, full life, rich with blessings. What a God! What a Guide!

PRAYER: Dear Father, thank You for the times You definitely led in times past. I claim the verse: "The Lord shall guide thee continually" as my personal verse for any future decisions I make. Amen.

59

And as ye would
that men should do to you,
do ye to them likewise.

Luke 6:31

24 God's Psychology

"She used psychology on him." "She was so tactful
in dealing with the uncooperative patient in Room 108.
That was a touchy situation." You've probably either
heard or made such remarks many times.

Treating others as we would like to be treated goes a
long way toward establishing a good relationship with
anyone, including the sarcastic patient.

Each individual from the least to the greatest needs to
feel loved, wanted, respected, and understood. When
any one of these essential needs is not met, the person is
susceptible to that calamity which is labeled by the
psychoanalyst as "inferiority complex." Such a person
may display various forms of distasteful behavior.

How will you deal with your sarcastic patient? Treat
him like you would hope to be treated if you were in his
circumstances. Be aware that there may be valid reasons
for his behavior. Some earlier emotional catastrophe
may have destroyed or scarred his self-image. He is probably battling his emotions and what he needs is a

Teach me to feel another's woe,
To hide the fault I see;
That mercy I to others show,
That mercy show to me.

Pope

sympathetic, listening ear. He could also stand a large dose of perceptive understanding. What he leaves unsaid is often more important than what he says. And don't forget to treat him as an intelligent person who is capable of understanding what is happening, even though he may be undergoing complicated tests and procedures.

So — be kind, be patient, be alert, and be compassionate. And use the opportunity to point out that every individual has worth in God's sight and that God has a plan for each of us. God also understands our needs and, what is more important, stands ready to help us with all of our troublesome situations.

Use God's psychology to understand and touch the life of that patient who only on the surface is gruff, ungrateful, and sullen.

PRAYER: Lord, help me to walk a mile in another's shoes before I condemn him. Forgive my hasty judgments and increase my love for others, sarcastic and unloving though they may be. Amen.

Most folks are about as happy
as they make up their minds to be.

Abraham Lincoln

25 God's Pharmacology

God wants us to be happy. Because He made us, He knows that joy and gladness are essential to our physical and emotional well-being. Adverse emotions cause ulcers, nervous disorders, colitis, cardiac problems, and hypertension. This is why God provided us with so many valuable instructions in this area.

With the help of a concordance I did a little research on what the Bible has to say about fear (King James Version):

6 texts say, "Be of good cheer."

21 texts say, "Be not afraid."

80 texts say, "Fear not."

God knows what fear does to the human body. This is why He repeated so often these words, "Fear not." You no doubt are well aware that the patient who goes to surgery very fearful and apprehensive is apt to come back to the recovery room in shock.

Many other helpful instructions are given to us for our benefit: "Rejoice in the Lord alway: and again I say, Rejoice" (Phil. 4:4); "Make a joyful noise unto the Lord, all ye lands. Serve the Lord with gladness: come before his presence with singing" (Ps. 100:1, 2); "Be strong and of a good courage" (Josh. 1:6).

God knows joy gives us strength. That's why He tells

A cheerful heart does good
like medicine,
but a broken spirit
makes one sick.

Prov. 17:22, TLB

us, "The joy of the Lord is your strength" (Neh. 8:10). When our hearts are full of joy, sadness and remorse have to flee. We can't have both at the same time. When courage comes in, fear leaves.

Jesus instructed His disciples to pray, "Forgive us our debts, as we forgive our debtors" (Matt. 6:12), because He knows that holding a grudge and harboring feelings of hatred toward someone will destroy happiness. We do well to heed this admonition, too.

God has also given man the wisdom to discover and distill life-saving drugs and medicines from plants (belladona, digitalis), animals (epinephrine, insulin, ACTH), and minerals (iodine, iron, epsom salt). In addition, man is able to produce chemically many healing substances.

PRAYER: Dear God, thank You for Your revelation of the importance of a cheerful heart. Help me always to strive to maintain a cheerful atmosphere for my patients, so they may recover more rapidly. Forgive me when I fail to do this. Thank You for the drugs and medicines You have made available. Help me to use them discreetly, under the orders of the physician. Amen.